ANOINTED
BLESSINGS

MICHAEL AND JULIE BATTAGLINI

ISBN 978-1-0980-2273-0 (paperback)
ISBN 978-1-0980-2274-7 (digital)

Christian Faith Publishing, Inc.
832 Park Avenue
Meadville, PA 16335
www.christianfaithpublishing.com

All scriptures, unless otherwise stated, are taken from the King James Version of the Holy Bible.

Cover art design by Jenaya Dawn Thibedeau and CFP

Printed in the United States of America

PREFACE

Thou preparest a table before me in the
presence of mine enemies: thou anointest
my head with oil; my cup runneth over
—Psalm 23:5

The kindness and love of our Saviour flow through every work
He establishes. He is motivated solely by His own goodness and willingness to pour grace upon grace through any and all who would
eat at His table, drink of His cup, and flow in His anointing. This
doesn't mean that our walk in this world is always meant to be pleasant, though. Our lives are seasonal and must be so in order for us to
grow. What it means is that when we yield to Him and cultivate a life
of obedience, all joys and all hardships become the means to a most
glorious end.

Julie and I have sought to move forward only as we are led and
have endeavored to maintain the purity and sincerity of this ministry,
even in the midst of our faults and weaknesses. We have been greatly
blessed as we have given ourselves to this process. Some of the mes-
sages in this book were written by Julie and some by me, but each has
been a gift unmerited and a treasure to be shared. When they were
all completed, they formed a panoramic picture of something very
precious the Lord wants to communicate to His Body.

This second book presents an image of what it means to walk
the Kingdom path, and it is, like the first, a depiction of the journey
of stewardship. Two years and twenty-five letters have produced this
vision. I felt we were to arrange this second set of letters chronologi-
cally, reflecting phases of spiritual growth, revelation, and experience

in the lives of God's people. Each message addresses another step, each step reveals another facet of His work, and each work revealed leads us closer to His heart. "For precept must be upon precept, precept upon precept; line upon line, line upon line; here a little, and there a little" (Isaiah 28:10).

Some steps are quite simple but contain essential instructions for our spiritual walk. Others are impartations of wisdom and power and deliver vital truths greatly needed at this hour. Still others had me breathless, even as I received them, for they seemed to carry me beyond who I am and will undoubtedly change your perception of who He is and who you are in His sight. Read each one slowly, deliberately, and repeatedly, and let Him kindle a fire within you to know and walk the higher path. Although these phases are presented in a particular order, the way He makes them known in your own life may vary to some extent. If given enough time, though, everyone who has purposed to give themselves to Him will experience them all to some degree.

Spirit Filled Blessings is a series of foundational truths about Kingdom life. *Anointed Blessings* follows a similar track but adds another dimension. To say that someone is filled with the Spirit is slightly different than saying that they, or the work that they do, is anointed. The two terms speak of the same reality, but the word *anointed* carries the sense that the person and the work are *set apart* by God. In Old Testament times, those who were anointed by the Lord had physical oil poured over them to signify that both they and the work they would do were sanctified by Him. That's what this book is. It's a collection of letters written and set apart by His leading for a specific application to a specific person, and that person is you. If we believe that God is all-knowing and all-powerful, then we may also surely know that every gift given by Him comes with His intimate awareness of each person who will receive and benefit from it. In other words, this is very personal.

The same Spirit who dwells in the two of us is seeking an audience with you. Will you open your heart to Him? We hope you will, that you may receive every message and every meaning He wishes to convey to you. As you turn the page to begin this journey with us, set yourself before Him as one who desires to grow in the understanding of your place in His heart and in His house. Cultivate the longing to be established in the revelation of His identity and yours. Seek not only to know but to be known by His voice. And remember, He is always deeply personal with you and is fully aware that this book has come into your hands for such a time as this.

In Christ,
Michael Battaglini

Blessings to you, my brothers and sisters in Christ.

Today's Scripture: Psalm 55:6

"And I said, 'Oh that I had wings like a dove! For then would I fly away and be at rest.'"

Today's Message: A Cry from the Depths

Have you ever allowed yourself to hope beyond the limitations of your earthly experience? Have you yet come to the place where your most passionate pursuits only leave you thirsting for something of true worth? Those who have detached from the pleasures and struggles of this life, long enough to search for something of substance, have taken their first step toward discovering what that substance is. All humanity reels under a veil that covers hearts and blinds perception, yet deep stirrings urge us to identify the inner ache we have sought so diligently to distract ourselves from. The longing to fly away and be at rest has been echoed through the ages by multitudes who have sensed that something more is waiting just beyond their sight.

The human experience is not as diverse as many believe it to be. Although we seek fulfilment in different ways, we have a common singular need that we strive to meet. Buried beneath years of suppression and neglect lies the consciousness of God and the awareness of our need for Him, for we each have a measure of revelation about who He is. "Because that which may be known of God is manifest in them; for God hath shewed it unto them" (Romans 1:19).

In our search for something to carry us beyond our deprived state, we have appealed to gods who can't save. We have looked to empty people to offer relief from our own emptiness. We have collected and consumed, built and dismantled, controlled and influenced until we have found ourselves exhausted and disillusioned. All the while we hold in our hearts the understanding of what God has shown us. It lies dormant, awaiting a spark of truth to ignite the flame of repentance. If you do not yet know Him, everything necessary to close the gap between your heart and His is available: the means to express the need within, the revelation of the One to whom you express it, and the wings of a Dove to carry you from your throne to His. "[t]oday if ye will hear His voice, harden not your hearts" (Hebrews 4:7b).

One day, the veil will be removed and every eye will see Him. "And He will destroy in this mountain the face of the covering cast over all people, and the veil that is spread over all nations" (Isaiah 25:7). The greatest testimony we can bring to the Lord on that day is not what we have done with *our* lives, but what we have done with the life He has offered us. Our walk with Him begins with a cry on our lips, reflecting an inner poverty so deep that if left to ourselves, we would lack even the ability to identify it. Yet, below our conscious thinking, a surge of necessity presses upward to pierce the veil. "Now when they heard this, they were pricked in their heart, and said unto Peter and to the rest of the apostles, 'Men and brethren, what shall we do'? Then Peter said unto them, 'Repent, and be baptized every one of you in the name of Jesus Christ for the remission of sins, and ye shall receive the gift of the Holy Ghost'" (Acts 2:37–38).

As we turn to Him, we are carried to a place of inner rest where we are fed and nourished in ways we haven't known. All who have tasted of this can testify of it. Allow Him to capture your attention. If you are His, take this as an offer to go deeper. If you are not His and your yearning for true life and love has been provoked beyond your ability to bear, cry out to God, turn to Him with all your heart, and let salvation begin its work in you.

Today's Prayer

God of all grace, I come to you today acknowledging that I am lost without you. I humble myself and confess that I have turned from you and gone my own way. Please forgive my sin according to your abundant mercy. I give myself to you today and ask that you would manifest yourself to me. In Jesus's name. Amen.

Blessings to you, my brothers and sisters in Christ.

Today's Scripture: Romans 10:12–13

"For there is no difference between the Jew and the Greek: for the same Lord over all is rich unto all that call upon Him. For whosoever shall call upon the name of the Lord shall be saved."

Today's Message: One Step Closer

Have you ever considered the heart that God has toward you? Have you ever opened yourself to the truth that you are loved without regard to personal merit and that He is willing to do all that is necessary to see you free? Each of us has in our hearts a cry for our Father and a yearning for a love without conditions. But humanity has turned from God, living and dying for religions and gods who offer what they cannot give, for our debt is too great. His answer to all our attempts at self-redemption was to become a man and to take our punishment upon Himself. Now His call goes forth to the ends of the earth to turn away from darkness and embrace the light. "For God so loved the world that He gave His only begotten Son, that whosoever believeth in Him should not perish, but have everlasting life" (John 3:16). This verse carries the weight of eternity upon itself. These simple words can transform everything that you are and change your life in a profound way if you will allow them to take root.

For those who belong to the Lord, salvation has taken its place at the center of our being and pulses outward in ever-increasing waves of glory until our whole lives are consumed by His light. Each new day holds fresh encounters with His grace and faithfulness that are just waiting to be discovered. Every sunrise can be met with the joyful anticipation of seeing works of freedom and deliverance unfold in very personal ways. The revelation of His tender love gives us the freedom to wrestle with Him, to plead for understanding, or to cry our hearts out if that's what we need to do. "O taste and see that the Lord is good: blessed is the man that trusteth in Him" (Psalm 34:8).

Just knowing that He is good will make us lighthearted as we go through our days. As our eyes are opened to see the work being done in us, our perception of His faithfulness will widen. We will rise to meet doubt and fear with a confidence we have never known. We will learn not to fear the unknown, for nothing is unknown to Him. "Fear thou not: for I am with thee: be not dismayed; for I am thy God: I will strengthen thee; yea, I will help thee; yea, I will uphold thee with the right hand of my righteousness" (Isaiah 41:10).

Pray for the grace to truly see Him that you may overflow with unwavering trust in His goodness. Take a moment to become aware of Him. Collect your thoughts and allow yourself to be open to the love freely offered. Focus on the Lord and let go of everything else. Be still. That stirring in your heart to know truth can and will be met by the one true God. Whether you are His or not, take one step closer today, and you will find that He is who He says He is. Come with a willingness to turn away from all that is darkness, and you will experience His love and mercy. He will not fail the one who calls upon His name.

Today's Prayer

Heavenly Father, I thank you for the grace and mercy that are freely offered to me. I choose to trust and believe in you. I choose to give myself to your truth which stands forever. I release my spirit to you and thank you for the love that I can find only as I draw near to you. In Jesus's name. Amen.

Blessings to you, my brothers and sisters in Christ.

Today's Scripture: Ezekiel 11:19,20

"And I will give them one heart, and I will put a new spirit within you; and I will take the stony heart out of their flesh, and will give them a heart of flesh. That they may walk in my statutes and keep mine ordinances and do them: and they shall be my people, and I will be their God."

Today's Message: Great Awakening of the Heart

What does it mean to have a heart after God? What does the Lord see when He looks upon His child, the one born of His Spirit? Before we were His, we were hardened in sin and slaves to our passions. When we cried out to Him in repentance, we expressed an awakening of a new and tenderized heart. "And because ye are sons, God hath sent forth the Spirit of His Son into your hearts, crying, 'Abba, Father'" (Galatians 4:6).

We have been made aware of the certainty of Scripture, and we now see ourselves and everything around us in the revelatory light of His presence. Because we have been given light and become the children of God, we find within ourselves a deep longing to live for Him. This is what now dwells at the core of our being. Our old way was to follow dark paths and to walk in rebellion, filled with destructive thoughts and rejection of all that was of God. Our fallen nature could only be changed by His power. "Create in me a clean heart, O God, and renew a right spirit within me" (Psalm 51:10).

By taking away our heart of stone and giving us a heart of flesh, He has made a way for us to walk boldly in the glory of His grace. He has caused us to draw near to Him and find fulfillment only in what comes from Him. "Blessed is the man whom thou choosest, and causest to approach unto thee, that he may dwell in thy courts:

we shall be satisfied with the goodness of thy house, even of thy holy temple" (Psalm 65:4).

Although our inner nature has been changed, we still must grow and shed the layers of our old identity that persist within us. Our Father works in many ways to bring us forth and mature us. He uses many avenues to humble and soften us and to encourage us in our love for Him. As we cooperate with Him and grow in His Word, people around us will see the transformation unfolding. They will see His character gradually replacing our former ways as our inward life grows to its full stature. "For which cause we faint not; but though our outward man perish, yet the inward man is renewed day by day" (2 Corinthians 4:16).

As the Lord combines His cleansing and purifying power with our obedience, our doubts and fears will fall from us one by one, and the inner work of His grace will flourish in our lives. Throughout Scripture, we see Him awakening those who are lost, replacing their emptiness with new vision, and filling their brokenness with His tender love. We have every reason to trust Him! To know God is to know His gentle, gracious love. As we yield to Him, we will become aware of how powerful He is in His work. We will discover that long before we even existed, His plans for us were already envisioned. He truly delights in the work of His hands.

Today's Prayer

Abba Father, as I stand before your throne of grace, I thank you for the spiritual awakening you have granted me. Fill me with your love and compassion as I release myself to you. My whole desire is to yield to the leading of your Spirit within me. I love you Lord, because you first loved me. In Jesus's name. Amen.

Blessings to you, my brothers and sisters in Christ.

Today's Scripture: Acts 1:8

"But ye shall receive power, after that the Holy Ghost is come upon you: and ye shall be witnesses unto me both in Jerusalem, and in all Judaea, and in Samaria, and unto the uttermost part of the earth."

Today's Message: The Witness of the Indwelling Spirit

How does the Spirit of God manifest His presence and work in you? How have you grown in your relationship with Him and in your sensitivity to His leading? Throughout Scripture, we find testimonies of His work, ministry, and power in and through His people. What He has revealed about Himself in His Word is true of Him still. He exists from eternity, unfolding the mysteries of God to all Creation. He is perfectly holy, all-knowing, and all-powerful, is eternally loving, merciful, and just, and dwells in Heaven, on Earth, and in the heart of every believer. "For there are three that bear record in Heaven, the Father, the Word, and the Holy Ghost; and these three are one. And there are three that bear witness in Earth, the Spirit, and the water, and the blood: and these three agree in one. If we receive the witness of men, the witness of God is greater: for this is the witness of God which He hath testified of His Son. He that believeth on the Son of God hath the witness in himself" (1 John 5:7–10a).

The work of the Spirit is to lead us into all truth and to reveal the heart of the Father. All gifts, callings, graces, and miracles flow forth from Him to glorify Christ. When we yield to Him, we are empowered to perform acts greater than our natural capabilities would allow us to. When the Body of Christ comes together in unity, the demonstration of His power is increased mightily. "And when they had prayed, the place was shaken where they were assembled together; and they were all filled with the Holy Ghost, and they spake the word of God with boldness. And the multitude of them that believed were of one heart and of one soul…" (Acts 4:31, 32a).

Walking in the fellowship and guidance of the Spirit should be our deepest longing, but sometimes our hearts grow dull and our ears become deaf. If we find ourselves in this state, it's important that we come to Him, believing in His grace and deep desire to bring us back to where we need to be. As we allow His direction to take hold again, we will be led through the narrow, rough areas and brought back into His rest and design for us. "Howbeit when He, the Spirit of truth, is come, He will guide you into all truth…" (John 16:13a).

How do we become consistently led and empowered by the Spirit? We must first set our hearts on things above that our minds may be renewed by His truth. We will find rest for our souls as we learn to recognize His promptings. Our attitudes and actions will be transformed, and His grace will overflow with abundant provision. Everything given to us to mature should be acted on that we may grow as extensions of the one who bears witness to all mankind. "But as it is written, eye hath not seen, nor ear heard, neither have entered into the heart of man, the things which God hath prepared for them that love Him. But God hath revealed them unto us by His Spirit: for the Spirit searcheth all things, yea, the deep things of God" (1 Corinthians 2:9,10).

Today's Prayer

Abba Father, I thank you for your mighty power that dwells within me. It is only through the communion of your Spirit that I find peace and joy in this life. As you reveal your way for me each day, I give you alone all glory, honor, and praise. In Jesus's name. Amen.

Blessings to you, my brothers and sisters in Christ.

Today's Scripture: Psalm 119:105

"Thy Word is a lamp unto my feet, and a light unto my path."

Today's Message: Light for the Journey

Do you ever feel that life is too noisy and full of demands and distractions? Stress and concerns have a way of flooding our thinking and bearing down on us until we're not even sure which way we're going. Sometimes choices present themselves so quickly that we have little time to weigh them. So we go with our gut, we do the things we have to do, and at the end of the day, it seems that all we have left is tomorrow's list.

When we're overwhelmed with daily burdens, it can be beneficial to step back and assess what we can do without. Taking inventory of our lives and removing what is unnecessary will give us much needed breathing space to allow the light of God to shine in our hearts. Our Father will pour out all the grace needed to stand joyfully in the midst of trials as we take time to fill ourselves with His Word.

Looking to Him for peace and direction will come naturally as we make it our habit to be still in His presence and meditate on Scripture. To *meditate* is simply to reflect on a verse or a passage repeatedly, visualizing it, and letting its meaning sink into us by His Spirit. Fix your thoughts on what is true, good, and right, and think on those things throughout your day. You will discover great peace when you consistently focus your physical and spiritual eyes on His truth. "Finally, brethren, whatsoever things are true, whatsoever things are honest, whatsoever things are just, whatsoever things are pure, whatsoever things are lovely, whatsoever things are of good report; if there be any virtue, and if there be any praise, think on these things" (Philippians 4:8).

Find a quiet place where you can be still. Ask the Lord to bring to mind a passage that He would have you to focus on, and allow His Spirit within you to make it personal to you. If you are His child, it already applies to you. All that is needed is a willingness to allow Him to bring that message home to your heart. Do this consistently, and you will find yourself walking in all the strength needed to fight the good fight of faith. As you become receptive to more and more of His Word, you will find that you walk with confidence and lightheartedness in the midst of adversity. Even *one* of His promises, if taken to heart, can cause us to walk above much of what we struggle with. His power will mingle with our faith and cause our souls to become increasingly purified. We will discover a supernatural wisdom that strengthens, guides, and gives hope in every situation. "I rejoice at thy Word, as one that findeth great spoil" (Psalm 119:162).

The way to know God and His will is to meditate on who He is, what He says about you, and what He is saying to you. If you want to be certain of His perspective on something, find passages that deal with the situation at hand and consciously choose to live in the light of them. Over time, you will discover that your whole outlook has been renewed and you will rejoice in the liberty and strength that you find. "Thy words were found, and I did eat them; and thy Word was unto me the joy and rejoicing of mine heart: for I am called by thy name, O Lord God of hosts" (Jeremiah 15:16).

Today's Prayer

Heavenly Father, I thank you for this time alone with you. Search me and know me that I may embrace your promises. Help me as I consider your Word and seek to live by it that I may surrender everything I am to you. In Jesus's name. Amen.

Blessings to you, my brothers and sisters in Christ.

Today's Scripture: Psalm 48:14

"For this God is our God for ever and ever: He will be our guide even unto death."

Today's Message: The Sure Hand That Guides

Do you ever have days where you feel like you're being tossed around by competing demands and there seems to be no meaning in any of it? Do you sometimes find yourself struggling to see the Lord's hand as you're faced with mounting troubles and disturbances? Although we don't always recognize it, stress and pressures take on a voice of their own, subtly suggesting that He has ceased to provide and that we must take matters into our own hands. We must be vigilant to cast down these imaginations or they will cause us to doubt His Word and promises. He always provides and is not negligent to help us in our time of need. It is only our perception that changes, never His guidance.

We all have two forces that seek preeminence within us. Fallen human nature seeks to be enthroned, in control, and governing our affairs. But we also have a deep knowledge that it is unwise to function this way. A cry rises from deep in our spirits for the Lord to direct our steps, order our lives, and lift us beyond the sure and soon termination of this life. This cry comes by the Spirit of God, the Spirit of adoption, melding with our hearts and calling out for restoration and direction. "For as many as are led by the Spirit of God, they are the sons of God. For ye have not received the spirit of bondage again to fear; but ye have received the Spirit of adoption, whereby we cry, Abba, Father" (Romans 8:14–15).

It's important to make a distinction between the voice of the Spirit and the voice of our old nature. Yielding to that nature will only leave us hollow inside. We are no longer slaves to the power of the Fall, so all attempts to live according to the flesh will leave us feeling unfulfilled. We must embrace the yearning within for the strong, guiding hand of our Father and have faith in His tender concern for our well-being.

Our victory is found through revelation. It is found when our hunger for God connects with the awareness that He will provide everything needed to answer that hunger. We only stumble when we're driven to answer legitimate needs in illegitimate ways. He may allow us to attempt this course for a season until we have exhausted ourselves in it, but let us not waste precious time struggling to do things our own way. The road can become smoother and more peaceful, even in the midst of trials, if we allow His peace to be our guide. "And let the peace of God rule in your hearts, to the which also ye are called in one body; and be ye thankful" (Colossians 3:15). Learn to detect the inward witness of the Spirit, even in small decisions, and He will take you where you need to go.

The Father will always hold His children, whether we're following His lead or not. We must trust that He has us, even in our immaturity. When we submit to His course, we align ourselves with everything we were created to be, and we taste of victory and peace. When we veer off track, reaching for what has not been given, He still holds us, but our lives become directionless and dull. Come to Him with a sincere heart, asking for the removal of everything that hinders His best for you, for He will withhold nothing that is beneficial. Let us go higher, reaching out with a desire to be led that we may connect with His desire to lead.

Today's Prayer

I thank you, Lord, that you help me to see above my struggles and walk in union with your everlasting guidance. I desire to give myself to you in all things that I may rest in your presence and delight in your goodness. In Jesus's name. Amen.

Blessings to you, my brothers and sisters in Christ.

Today's Scripture: Colossians 3:1

"If ye then be risen with Christ, seek those things which are above, where Christ sitteth on the right hand of God."

Today's Message: In Silent Reflection

Have you ever reflected on the wonders of God's plan for you in this turbulent world? We all go through periods where we feel unstable because of challenging or unpredictable circumstances. We have all been influenced, even consumed by earthly cares and distractions. At any given time, seasons can change, our lives can become something we haven't seen before, and all our striving to maintain familiarity can be shown to be in vain. Our Father speaks to us with tenderness: "Love not the world, neither the things that are in the world. If any man love the world, the love of the Father is not in him. For all that is in the world, the lust of the flesh, and the lust of the eyes, and the pride of life, is not of the Father, but of the world. And the world passeth away, and the lust thereof: but he that doeth the will of God abideth forever" (1 John 2:15–17).

God's temporal provision is a gift to us that we may be without care and free to pursue His best in the Kingdom. Today is the day to gather our affections and priorities and set them on the Lord and on His eternal purposes. We are offered so very much, and as we seek His pleasure in all that we do, we will find that our vision and focus are lifted above the pain and commotion of this fallen realm.

God has appointed a time for everything under Heaven. Every mystery in His heart is revealed in the season He has ordained. You were specifically chosen to bring forth part of His eternal plan. Each of His creations that you see has their own time too. Everything He has made has deep meaning and purpose to its existence, especially man, who is brought forth into eternity. His desire for us is evident in Scripture. He calls upon the redeemed to be His redeemers in the earth. "Thus saith God the Lord, He that created the heavens, and stretched them out; He that spread forth the earth, and that which cometh out of it; He that giveth breath unto the people upon it, and spirit to them that walk therein: I the Lord have called thee in righteousness, and will hold thine hand, and will keep thee and give thee for a covenant of the people, for a light of the Gentiles; To open the blind eyes, to bring out the prisoners from the prison, and them that sit in darkness out of the prison house" (Isaiah 42:5–7).

Let us reconcile, restore, and forgive that we may know the love of God. Let us reflect on all the ways He has shown His kindness to us that we may show it to others. Acknowledge and embrace the truth that His purposes for you did not end but began at the cross. They did not end on the day of your salvation either but will blossom into their full realization as you give yourself to them. Allow this moment to be the one where you put the things of this world behind you and ask the Lord to lead the way. He has determined when it all begins and ends. A time of silent reflection is not wasted. It is a precious time with God.

Today's Prayer

Abba Father, in this time of silence in your presence, I thank you for giving me a chance to reflect on what I value most. Everything I do and have comes from you. Nothing you give can I boast about. I can only receive and be thankful. You gave it all to me, and this day, I give my all to you. In Jesus's name. Amen.

Blessings to you, my brothers and sisters in Christ.

Today's Scripture: 2 Timothy 2:13

"If we believe not, yet He abideth faithful: He cannot deny Himself."

Today's Message: He Abides Faithful

Do you struggle to trust God during periods of tribulation and trial? Do you long for a faith that will stand strong, no matter the circumstances? Sometimes seasons of difficulty in our journey and faltering in our faith are what lead to a strong and unshakable confidence in Him. This is why we will sometimes be allowed to pass through the very things we fear that He may show Himself strong and sufficient on our behalf.

The Lord will finish the work He has started within us. His promises to His children are not undone by our failings or shortcomings or even by our wavering trust that He will do what He has promised. His work of salvation is so thorough, His act of adoption so complete, that our confidence need not rest in the work of our hands or the convictions of our heart. All He requires is that we bring everything we are and everything we are not to Him, steadfastly dedicating ourselves to His course for our lives. "Wherefore seeing we also are compassed about with so great a cloud of witnesses, let us lay aside every weight, and the sin which doth so easily beset us, and let us run with patience the race that is set before us, looking unto Jesus, the author and finisher of our faith; who for the joy that was set before Him endured the cross, despising the shame, and is set down at the right hand of the throne of God" (Hebrews 12:1–2). The Lord Himself is the author and finisher of our faith. It is enough for us to know the next step and to take it in obedience. It is enough for us to embrace what is revealed about the unique and specific plan He has envisioned for us.

Our Father is always there to relieve our fears, provide for our needs, and uphold us when we stumble. His unrelenting commitment to us is the divine pen with which He authors our walk of faith in this world. Once our eyes are opened to this truth we can stand, not on our devotion to Him, but on His faithfulness to us. The Kingdom He is building, using flawed and broken people, is neither flawed nor broken. How can this be, unless the power and the work are entirely His? He has designed a plan for each of His children that takes into account every victory and every failure we will have throughout our walk in this world. Our identity in Christ is already written in Heaven and on our spirits, and only that which has been authored from eternity will remain for eternity. "Forasmuch as ye are manifestly declared to be the epistle of Christ ministered by us, written not with ink, but with the Spirit of the living God; not in tables of stone, but in fleshy tables of the heart. And such trust have we through Christ to God-ward: Not that we are sufficient of ourselves to think anything as of ourselves; but our sufficiency is of God" (2 Corinthians 3:3–5).

As you stand before the power and love of your divine Author, allow yourself to set aside the burdens that weigh down your heart. They seem so real and so threatening, but they are not. You need only to alter your perspective enough to know that He abides faithful when you wrestle with doubts and fears. You need only to know that He makes provision as any good father would, even when your problems seem to overshadow your faith. This knowledge in you is the ink with which He pens yet another verse in the epistle of your trust-walk and another stone by which you build yourself up on your most holy faith.

Today's Prayer

Father, I come to you standing on your promise that you will forever abide faithful to me. I thank you that I need not fear when troubles come, for you can and will show yourself to be the answer to my every need. In Jesus's name. Amen.

Blessings to you, my brothers and sisters in Christ.

Today's Scripture: Psalm 40:2

"He brought me up also out of a horrible pit, out of the miry clay, and set my feet upon a rock, and established my goings."

Today's Message: Released and Established

Do you have a testimony of the saving power of God? Can you look back on where you came from and point to a time when you were released from darkness and despair and set on solid ground? He is many things to His people, but what He first proves Himself to be is our deliverer. We were all born into bondage, we have all entered the world sold under sin, and we have all been in dire need of rescue. Not only has a way been made for us to be born into His Kingdom, but we have been offered a journey of increasing freedom and peace as we mature.

Our deliverance was not a one-time event. We were not birthed into the heavenly Kingdom only to be left in our earthly bondages. The Lord leads us forward from season to season and from glory to glory. Our enemies are driven out one by one to make way for the expansion of His nature within us. Sometimes the process is painful, sometimes pleasant, but each work is done in perfect wisdom and for our highest good, culminating in the resurrection of our bodies and the restoration of the earth. "Because the creation itself also shall be delivered from the bondage of corruption into the glorious liberty of the children of God. For we know that the whole creation groaneth and travaileth in pain together until now. And not only they, but ourselves also, which have the firstfruits of the Spirit, even we ourselves groan within ourselves, waiting for the adoption, to wit, the redemption of our body" (Romans 8:21–23).

God's promise to us is that if we have tasted of deliverance, we will, in due course, experience it in its fullness. "If the Son therefore shall make you free, ye shall be free indeed" (John 8:36). A unique plan has been prepared for each of us. We are all different and have come from different backgrounds. We each need specific facets of His grace in order to grow into the people we are called to be, and only He knows what each person requires. We have not only been pulled from the pit, but as the psalmist wrote, He has established our goings. We have been made to move forward into the fulfillment of everything we will become in Him. To walk in His perfect will, we must cooperate with Him as we are brought forward. We must go to Him before every step to determine if that step is indeed from Him.

It is impossible to come into contact with the renewing power of God and remain the same. Just a touch from His mighty hand brings new life and fresh hope; and the more we yield, the freer we will be. He will go before us and bring revelatory light to everything we are to do. As we obey and walk in consistent obedience, new avenues will open up and power will overflow to touch the lives of those around us. This is how His Body grows. This is how the enemy is pushed back and new claims for the Kingdom are staked. His life and divine nature are built up within us and poured out again and again until exponential waves of growth and glory form up the holy temple He has ordained from eternity.

Today's Prayer

Lord, I know you are my deliverer. I know I am yours and that you are ever willing and able to pull me out of every snare and present me before your throne of grace perfectly free. I thank you, Father, that there is no area of my heart that will be left unchanged as I give myself to you. In Jesus's name. Amen.

Blessings to you, my brothers and sisters in Christ.

Today's Scripture: John 4:23,24

"But the hour cometh, and now is, when the true worshippers shall worship the Father in spirit and in truth; for the Father seeketh such to worship Him. God is Spirit, and they that worship Him must worship Him in spirit and in truth."

Today's Message: Adoration in His Presence

What is the significance of worship in your life? Is it your language of affection to God? Is it a manifestation of His love flowing through you? Is it a place of refuge for your soul? It can be all of these and so much more, for it is the ultimate communication to God of our absolute devotion to Him. It is an intertwining of our hearts with His that declares our relationship with Him to be more important than anything, even His favor and the victory that we find in His name. In essence, to worship God is to invite Him to search the deepest part of us. By His grace, we can grow into a total commitment of spirit, soul, and body so that our worship truly becomes the language of a life dedicated to Him. "I beseech you therefore, brethren, by the mercies of God, that ye present your bodies a living sacrifice, holy, acceptable unto God, which is your reasonable service" (Romans 12:1).

Our expressions of love for the Lord are based on the revelation of who He is. Knowing *what* we know isn't enough without knowing *who* we know. Mental knowledge alone will not stir us to search out the mysteries of His nature or bring us to a place of adoration in His presence, but as we look upon Him by the empowerment of the Spirit, He will be made known to us. To go deeper in the things of the Kingdom, we must have a mind solely centered on Him and renewed by the truth of Scripture. "And be not conformed to this world: but be ye transformed by the renewing of your mind, that ye may prove what is that good, and acceptable, and perfect will of God" (Romans 12:2).

Part of loving Him involves having our hearts in tune with His and our minds renewed by the Word of His grace. As we reflect on His glory and on the glory of the work being done within us, praise will bubble up and flow out of us without thought. His kindness will be our mainstay and our joy, and we will know the peace and security that is found only in a deep connection with Him.

When we release ourselves in praise and gratitude to our Father, we are saying that we trust Him to provide everything our souls are longing for. We are saying that we believe He will graciously choose better for us than we would for ourselves. Our greatest reward comes as we learn to relate to Him from the very center of our being, longing to hear His voice and be led by His will. "But as it is written, eye hath not seen, nor ear heard, neither have entered into the heart of man, the things which God hath prepared for them that love Him. But God hath revealed them unto us by His Spirit: for the Spirit searcheth all things, yea, the deep things of God" (1 Corinthians 2:9,10).

His heart will be revealed to us, we will be led from glory to glory, and we will be empowered to express gratitude in ways we could never do on our own. Let us come to Him in faith, believing that He will provide everything needed to glorify Him with all that we are.

Today's Prayer

Abba Father, I rejoice for the privilege of worshipping you in spirit and in truth. I thank you for the times when my heart is intertwined with yours and we are one. I exalt your mighty name. May it be lifted up on high this day as I give myself fully to you. In Jesus's name. Amen.

Blessings to you, my brothers and sisters in Christ.

Today's Scripture: Psalm 118:22–24

"The stone which the builders refused is become the head stone of the corner. This is the Lord's doing; it is marvelous in our eyes. This is the day which the Lord hath made; we will rejoice and be glad in it."

Today's Message: Morning Revelations

Did you know that everything God has created reflects and reveals glorious truths about His nature and ways? Have you ever considered that He has woven prophetic statements into and throughout all Creation? The sun, the moon, the stars, and every living creature on Earth speak forth the parables of His Kingdom. The morning sunrise declares perhaps the greatest of all mysteries: God became man, was rejected that we would be accepted, and has established a new day in which His morning stars already shine in the darkness.

"But unto you that fear my name shall the Sun of righteousness arise with healing in His wings; and ye shall go forth, and grow up as calves of the stall" (Malachi 4:2). The dawn of the Kingdom of God on Earth is infinitely more glorious than any earthly sunrise that mirrors it. The light from Heaven that has shone in our hearts is but a faint glimmer compared to the glory that is coming. His light within us foretells a great deliverance that will soon cover the earth. We have barely glimpsed the power and glory that will be released as the new morning breaks forth and His people are liberated from the bondage of corruption. We have tasted of the firstfruits of His Spirit, of healing, of peace, and of freedom. We have rejoiced in His light and made a place in our lives for His testimonies. He desires to pour out much more upon us. He would have us to prepare a greater place, cultivating a deep longing for the increase of His government and peace, both in ourselves and in His corporate Body. We must choose to believe that we are able, by the grace provided, to remove the clutter of this empty, passing world that our hearts would be enlarged and that we would take the Kingdom by force. The Sun of righteousness will arise over us and bring healing and nourishment as we yield each step of our journey to Him.

"The heavens declare the glory of God; and the firmament sheweth His handywork. Day unto day uttereth speech, and night unto night sheweth knowledge. There is no speech nor language, where their voice is not heard" (Psalm 19:1–3). The Lord has not hidden His testimonies from man. He will heal our eyes and our ears that in seeing, we may perceive and in hearing, we may understand. But perception and understanding bring greater accountability, so in His mercy, He will not revive our spiritual senses until a steadfast resolve to know and live in His will has been settled and established within us. He doesn't examine or take into account our natural abilities, for without Him, we can do nothing. He asks only for our trust and willingness. He provides everything else. He has already taken His place at the foundation of our lives as the chief cornerstone. We have already been translated into the new day. We are already His lights that shine in a dark place. We cannot add to or take away from the work that has been done. We can only take our place in it.

May the light of this new day be revealed to your eyes. May its truths sink deep into your ears. Continually return your attention to Him. Let the pure desire He has placed in you, the longing for all that is of Him, rise to press through everything that would hinder it. Your Father extends His heart, His hand, and His voice to you that you would know His heart, take hold of His hand, and hear His voice, "[w]hereunto ye do well that ye take heed, as unto a light that shineth in a dark place, until the day dawn, and the day star arise in your hearts" (2 Peter 1:19b).

Today's Prayer

Lord, I come before your throne of grace and thank you that I am free to rejoice in the light of the new day. I thank you that from eternity, you have ordained a place for me in the light, and I humbly come to you and ask that you would lead me into your perfect will for my life. In the mighty name of Jesus. Amen.

Blessings to you, my brothers and sisters in Christ.

Today's Scripture: Hebrews 12:22-23

"But ye are come unto mount Sion, and unto the city of the living God, the heavenly Jerusalem, and to an innumerable company of angels, to the general assembly and church of the firstborn, which are written in Heaven, and to God, the judge of all, and to the spirits of just men made perfect."

Today's Message: Kingdom Citizens

Do you hunger for a revelation that will see you through the rigors of daily life in this world? Have you ever meditated on the truth that your actual citizenship is in Heaven? This reality has the power to alter your entire way of thinking and living, for where you perceive your home to be, there will your heart be also.

Because we have been conditioned to settle for a lower existence, for the dull and the finite; we sometimes find it difficult to reach for the glorious and the infinite. Yet, this is what we have been given. We have been saved, not only *out of* a system of corruption and pain, but *into* the everlasting Kingdom of righteousness, peace, and joy. Living day-to-day can be so much more than heavy burdens and fleeting pleasures. We have come to a city whose light can dispel our every attachment to this fallen realm if we would but see it. In our lower state, in our blindness, we were mere cogs in a machine that grinds on in toil and emptiness. This is the condition of all who have their portion in this life. We are told that this is the most we can expect or hope for, but the light of the eternal city has shone in our hearts, and it beckons us higher.

"By faith Abraham, when he was called to go out into a place which he should after receive for an inheritance, obeyed; and he went out, not knowing whither he went. By faith he sojourned in the land of promise, as in a strange country, dwelling in tabernacles with Isaac and Jacob, the heirs with him of the same promise: For he looked for a city which hath foundations, whose builder and maker is God" (Hebrews 11:8–10). As children of Abraham, we too have come to a place that we will receive as an inheritance. We too are called to lay down our hope for a man-made temporal system that will accommodate our faith in God and embrace a city not made by hands, whose builder and maker *is* God. We are not called to help build or uphold any earthly government or system, for our hope is not in this world any longer. The Kingdom of God must be established in the hearts and lives of individual people, for the spiritual atmosphere of our nation cannot be changed any other way.

"Ye are all the children of light, and the children of the day: we are not of the night, nor of darkness" (1 Thessalonians 5:5). Because His Spirit bears witness with our spirit and testifies that we are His children, we are free to receive all He has said about the realm we have been born into. Can you sense the light of His glory shining out from the center of your being? That is who you are: A Kingdom citizen. You are not anything you have achieved in any Earth-bound institution nor are you any other badge, title, or office awarded to you by man. You are forever a child of the light and of the day. He will bring you forward and show you all you need to see about your true identity. For now, you need only rest in the light of His presence and know that you have been brought to your everlasting home.

Today's Prayer

Father, I thank you that my identity in you will stand forever and that my name is written in Heaven. I remove my affections from this fallen world and fix them upon you, for you are the light of the glorious eternal city that I have been brought to. In Jesus's name. Amen.

Blessings to you, my brothers and sisters in Christ.

Today's Scripture: Ephesians 3:17–19

"That Christ may dwell in your hearts by faith, that ye, being rooted and grounded in love may be able to comprehend with all saints what is the breadth, and length, and depth, and height; And to know the love of Christ, which passeth knowledge, that ye might be filled with all the fullness of God."

Today's Message: Grounded in Faith with Passion

Is your faith anchored in the revelation of God's faithfulness? When we're standing in the full awareness of His unfailing love, we show that we have allowed the truth of Scripture to move from our physical eyes to our spiritual eyes. Our hope need never be suppressed by the confusion and fears around us. Only He understands the design beneath our circumstances, and it will be revealed to those who learn the lessons and mysteries of faith.

Our Father has extended precious promises to us, and we can rest in the fact that they will be fulfilled in His time. This knowledge frees us to allow our daily walk with Him to be filled with expectant gratitude. We need not be subject to reason and opinions about what faith is. It is only important that we know what it is in us. How well do you know your Father in Heaven? Who is He that lives within you? These are the questions that only a true, living faith can answer.

We are all subject to trials and challenges, but gaining an accurate perception of God in the midst of them is the key to standing in confidence before Him. Without exception, spiritual valleys are inevitable, but His unwavering presence is always with us when we feel vulnerable. "Yea, though I walk through the valley of the shadow of death, I will fear no evil: for thou art with me; thy rod and thy staff, they comfort me" (Psalm 23:4). In the midst of difficulties, our trust in God is being tested in a most crucial way that we may learn that He is the only one who can provide comfort and assurance through it all. Faith needs to be both rested in and tried that we may recognize His constancy in our lives. "My Father, which gave them me, is greater than all; and no man is able to pluck them out of my Father's hand" (John 10:29).

It isn't our natural abilities that empower us to live the life we're called to. It's obedience to His leading and empowerment that brings victory. We tend to limit ourselves to what we can do, but we were created and designed with no boundaries or hindrances as we walk in obedience. God is greater than all our human limitations, and in Him, we're complete, equipped, and lacking nothing. The ultimate success is to not let the fear of failure hinder you. It's not about what you can do. It's about what you have been called to do and who you are in Him. So stand on a foundation of confidence and assurance that He is greater in all things.

What fills our faith with passion? Commitment, obedience, and time will build a reservoir of experiences with God, filling us with great joy and anticipation. As we move forward, many layers of depth and richness will be added to us, and we will grow to be consumed by His grace and kindness.

Today's Prayer

Abba Father, I bless your name in spirit and in truth. I thank you, Father, that my hope in you is grounded in the awareness of your goodness. You are the source of all life, and I hold on to you. You have all power and authority to fulfill what you have called me to for a great harvest to come. In Jesus's name. Amen.

Blessings to you, my brothers and sisters in Christ.

Today's Scripture: 1 Peter 5:10

"But the God of all grace, who hath called us unto His eternal glory by Christ Jesus, after that ye have suffered a while, make you perfect, establish, strengthen, and settle you."

Today's Message: The Greater the Call, the Deeper the Work

Have you grown to the place where you seek the will of the Lord in all that you do? Has your heart been moved by the Spirit to know your calling and the gifts He has put within you? The course He has plotted for your life carries with it the power of transformation. It will do a deep work in your heart. It will draw people to Him and bring forth the person you were created to be. We have all been given spiritual gifts that will bear eternal fruit, but we must activate what we have been given. We must become united with Him in what He reveals about Himself and about our identity in the Kingdom. "And [we] have put on the new man, which is renewed in knowledge after the image of Him that created him" (Colossians 3:10).

The willingness to seek the Lord and to find our place in His house will bring His plans to bear upon us. He will work a deep passion in our hearts that will often invite greater challenges than we can handle on our own. But the intensity of our trials will never outweigh the abundant grace provided to walk through them. We will be sustained and brought into greater levels of His peace as we remain committed to moving forward. As we walk with Him in the way that He chooses, His character and nature will be reflected in increasing measure through us. When we stumble, He will not take back what He has given but will use our weaknesses to do an even deeper work within us. "For the gifts and the calling of God are without repentance" (Romans 11:29).

Each new avenue of growth will come with unforeseen challenges that are allowed by Him that we might walk forward in faith and unlock the mysteries of His wisdom and power. The passion and anticipation that arises within us as we walk, along with our awareness of the specific way in which we are anointed, will bring us into new realms of glory and revelation. He will use our gifts to open new doors and create new horizons in our lives that we may ascend to new heights in our relationship with Him. "A man's gift maketh room for him, and bringeth him before great men" (Proverbs 18:16).

Embrace the motivation within you to walk in obedience. That hunger in your heart has come only from the hand of God, and it arises from an ordained, specific, eternal purpose that dwells in the mysteries of His heart. To know Him is to know His ways and to have the faith to walk and live in them. His will and direction for you will always become evident when they are met with your willingness and faith. As you respond to His call, He will pour out favor in such measure that you will not have room enough to contain it.

Today's Prayer

Abba Father, I thank you for the gifts and calling you have bestowed upon me. You have poured out your Spirit and unending grace so many times and in so many ways. Lead me deeper in my relationship with you and in your plans for my life. All of this is indeed a gift from you, and I rejoice in the greatness of your heart. In Jesus's mighty name. Amen.

Blessings to you, my brothers and sisters in Christ.

Today's Scripture: Psalm 119:37

"Turn away mine eyes from beholding vanity; and quicken thou me in thy way."

Today's Message: The Way of Transformation

Have you experienced the renewing power of God? Have you witnessed the divine nature within you expanding outward and touching every part of your life? What has been offered to us in His resurrection is nothing less than a total transformation of all that we are. His salvation reaches to the very core of our being and consumes us from the inside out. His desire and plan is to cause us to walk above the influences of this world in the realms of the Spirit. "Whereby are given unto us exceeding great and precious promises: that by these ye might be partakers of the divine nature, having escaped the corruption that is in the world through lust" (2 Peter 1:4).

The more we give ourselves to the Lord and to His plans for our lives, the more we will walk in the manifestation of His divine character. If we're to live in the victory that has been offered to us, we must be increasingly selective about what we give our time and attention to. Make it your passion to know which things to focus on, which words to abide by, and which people to spend your time with. If we set our hearts to desire the glories of His Kingdom in our midst, we will find out quickly that the things of this world do not satisfy. "If ye then be risen with Christ, seek those things which are above, where Christ sitteth on the right hand of God. Set your affection on things above, not on things on the earth. For ye are dead, and your life is hid with Christ in God. When Christ, who is our life, shall appear, then shall ye also appear with Him in glory" (Colossians 3:1–4).

Learning and walking God's redemptive path is the answer to our deepest needs and longings, but not every option that comes our way is from Him. Some choices that are presented are distractions to try to pull us off course. Seek Him for discernment that you may know if what is competing for your attention is designed by Him to further His work. If it isn't, ask for the grace and wisdom to set it aside, and He will be faithful to help you. "Prove all things; hold fast that which is good" (1 Thessalonians 5:21).

We must cultivate a steadfast resolve to run the race that is set before us. Spending our time on what He has put in front of us is truly fulfilling, and it will give place to His transformative power. If we fix our gaze on Him and let go of distractions and the need for man's approval, we will see layer upon layer of His kindness and provision unfolding before our eyes. He will confirm each work that He is doing, both in us and through us. Sometimes it will be apparent before it begins, sometimes during the process, and sometimes after it is completed, but He *will* confirm it. Our hearts will be enlarged with joy and satisfaction as we witness one piece after another of our eternal self and the eternal Kingdom being set in place by Him.

It is liberating to learn the way of transformation, to learn what God is doing and what He is not. It removes the burden of empty choices and the regret of wrong paths. The release that comes from the realization of His work in you can only be experienced. It cannot be told. So focus on Him, walk in obedience, and you will live in the peace and fulfilment of His glorious plan.

Today's Prayer

Father, I thank you for ordering my steps. I thank you for planning good things for me and helping me to discern what is from you and what is not. I pray you would help me to avoid distractions as I focus my heart and mind on you. I rejoice to behold your power as you bring me from glory to glory. In Jesus's name. Amen.

Blessings to you, my brothers and sisters in Christ.

Today's Scripture: Psalm 126:6

"For as the rain cometh down, and the snow from Heaven, and returneth not thither, but watereth the earth and maketh it bring forth and bud, that it may give seed to the sower and bread to the eater, so shall my word be that goeth forth out of my mouth: it shall not return unto me void, but it shall accomplish that which I please, and it shall prosper in the thing whereto I sent it" (Isaiah 55:10, 11).

Today's Message: Sow the Word, Reap the Kingdom

Did you know that there are eternal purposes of God that only find their fulfillment through sowing and reaping? Although this process has an earthly application, it is but a reflection of a glorious heavenly reality. The everlasting seed is the Word of God. "Being born again, not of corruptible seed, but of incorruptible, by the Word of God, which liveth and abideth forever" (1 Peter 1:23). Those who receive it into their hearts will see the fruit of righteousness spring forth in due time. Those who learn how to sow it will see the Kingdom of God manifested in power and glory.

This world is experiencing seasons of increasing turmoil. Desperate conditions and rapidly changing standards seem to be more and more the norm. Tribulations in the earth are causing many to cry out for answers and for action. Our answer and our action must be that we stand united as the Body of Christ and that we extend the hope of Scripture, both to one another and to the lost. What has been given to us must be given out, for He "hath reconciled us to Himself by Jesus Christ, and hath given to us the ministry of reconciliation" (2 Corinthians 5:18b). We will witness the light of faith and hope dispelling the darkness and despair around us as we learn to walk in the daily disciplines of His will. We will experience the advance of His Kingdom among the people we influence as we learn the unique way He has gifted us to reveal His truth.

The Word of God does not return to Him void. It prospers in the hearts that embrace it and it brings forth spiritual life in abundance. If we learn to be led by the Spirit to deliver the right words at the right time, we will find great fulfillment in our obedience. "A man hath joy by the answer of his mouth: and a word spoken in due season, how good is it" (Proverbs 15:23)!

As we give ourselves to Him, we will learn to distinguish not only *what* He is saying, but also *how* and *when* to speak it. We will become passionate about sowing His Word when we recognize that it is bringing forth the Kingdom in our midst. As we partner with others of like mind and their gifts are joined with ours, power and joy will overflow. "And he that reapeth receiveth wages, and gathereth fruit unto life eternal: that both he that soweth and he that reapeth may rejoice together" (John 4:36).

As we see spiritual life manifesting in the people we minister to, we will know the value of our labors. Rejoice in the sowing time and let thoughts of an abundant harvest fill you with gratitude. In due season, you will reap in joy, for every seed sown by the leading of the Spirit brings forth a measure of turning to God. "Therefore, my beloved brethren, be ye steadfast, unmovable, always abounding in the work of the Lord, forasmuch as ye know that your labour is not in vain in the Lord" (1 Corinthians 15:58).

Today's Prayer

Father God, I thank you that you have put these desires within me and have stirred my heart to receive your Word and to sow it into the lives of others. Each and every soul is close to your heart, so lead the way as I pour out everything you have poured into me. In Jesus's name. Amen.

Blessings to you, my brothers and sisters in Christ.

Today's Scripture: Luke 4:22

"And all bare Him witness, and wondered at the gracious words which proceeded out of His mouth. And they said, 'Is not this Joseph's son'"?

Today's Message: The Gracious Offense

Have you learned to give place to the Spirit of God that His witness and voice might be manifested in you? Do you know how to recognize His promptings and stirrings in your spirit, indicating His desire to speak His heart into a situation? If you are part of the Body of Christ, you will be called upon to give testament to the unique facet of His likeness and anointing that you carry. He has given each of us a part of Himself, and we each bear a new name before Him. This reflection of His glory may cause confusion or even offense in those who know us. His voice and manner can sometimes seem foreign, even among His own, and especially to those who are *not* foreign to the person He is speaking through. All who seek to know and serve the Lord must one day face the question, "Is not this Joseph's son?" We will all be called to stand at the junction between Heaven and Earth where the power and grace of God meet the offense of familiarity.

"Wherefore henceforth know we no man after the flesh: yea, though we have known Christ after the flesh, yet now henceforth know we Him no more" (2 Corinthians 5:16). If the Lord chose to be clothed in flesh and to be seen as common and familiar, we shouldn't think it strange when He speaks and ministers through His people. We must trust Him enough to allow the free expression of His voice and nature, even as it confounds those who can't see past the yielded vessel. We must also be willing to lay down our own standards of measurement and judgment as He graciously ministers to *us* by the vessel of His choosing. Each time He moves, He has a purpose. Each time He speaks, He has a reason. Nothing is done in vain, and you will not be asked to surrender to what He is doing in you or in anyone else unless the result will be eternal. Relating to people based on their identity in Christ brings unity. Acknowledging that this is *not* Joseph's son, but one anointed by God to carry His authority and testimony, heralds the coming of the King and His Kingdom in our midst.

"But God hath chosen the foolish things of the world to confound the wise; and God hath chosen the weak things of the world to confound the things which are mighty; And base things of the world, and things which are despised, hath God chosen, yea, and things which are not, to bring to nought things that are: That no flesh should glory in His presence" (1 Corinthians 1:27–29). The gracious offense is a demonstration of His glory in His kindness. We are called to embrace those whom He has chosen to express this kindness through and to love them as He does. We are also called to embrace His way in our own lives as He reveals who He is and how He loves us. We cannot but stand in awe as we see the wisdom, might, and noble character of God flow through the one who has been despised for being foolish, weak, and base. His ways are higher than our ways. He perfectly accomplishes all that is right and good and displays His power and wisdom through us as an undeniable witness that every eye may see Him.

Today's Prayer

Father, I thank you for your willingness to extend your hand through me. I desire to see and receive you in any person you choose to make yourself known. I pray I would always have a willing heart to give you place whenever and however it pleases you to reveal yourself. In Jesus's name. Amen.

Blessings to you, my brothers and sisters in Christ.

Today's Scripture: Proverbs 29:25

"The fear of man bringeth a snare, but whoso putteth his trust in the Lord shall be safe."

Today's Message: Safe in His Hands

Do you struggle with the fear of rejection? Do you sometimes feel the need to keep others happy at all costs? We will always encounter people who try to pressure us into their mold. They may be friends, coworkers, or family, and they may mean well in their efforts. But if we try to feel safe through their acceptance, our conscience will increasingly object to the compromises that are expected of us.

No matter how close we are to people, and no matter what expectations they have of us, their favor cannot fill that empty place within us. The Lord seeks to bring us to the place where we are no longer overwhelmed by the words and actions of others and where we do not feel the need to change with every criticism. We can't make everyone happy, we can't make everyone like us, and we will surely never win over all our critics. Let this truth sink deep into your heart: Freedom will come as you learn to walk solely in the love and grace of your Father and in His revealed will for your life. He is the one who leads us to the place of true safety. He is the *only* one who can set us free from the fear of people and from the confinement of their opinions of us.

When you're being pressured to act against your conscience, take a deep breath, collect yourself, and become aware of His presence. Allow yourself to sense and trust in the sustaining power of the Spirit. "Oh how great is thy goodness, which thou hast laid up for them that fear thee; which thou hast wrought for them that trust in thee before the sons of men! Thou shalt hide them in the secret of thy presence from the pride of man: thou shalt keep them secretly in a pavilion from the strife of tongues" (Psalm 31:19–20). His peace and power will be a shield over your heart and mind as you let go and trust that you are safe in His love.

Ask the Lord to search your soul and reveal the root cause of your struggle. He desires a willingness to be transparent before Him. It's important to understand that our longing to be accepted isn't wrong, for we were not created to desire rejection. That's why we must renew our minds with the truth that He is greater, that He loves us freely, and that He is willing to meet us exactly where we are. He is there to help us, step by step, as we walk into freedom. The more focused you are on Him, the more you will find yourself unconcerned with the opinions of others.

If people don't understand your identity in Christ, it's okay. If you lose some friends along the way because you wouldn't let them divert you from His path, they weren't your true friends anyway. You don't need the approval of man; you only need your Father's approval, and you have it, because when He looks at you, He sees you as complete in Christ. Keep your heart filled with truth, hide yourself in the secret of His presence, give yourself to His course for your life, and you will experience freedom. "The name of the Lord is a strong tower: the righteous runneth into it, and is safe" (Proverbs 18:10).

Today's Prayer

Father God, I humbly come to you and invite you to search my heart and soul. Let my ways be pleasing to you. Let my thoughts be your thoughts. I thank you for walking with me every step of the way. I thank you for bringing me into a place of rest as I learn just how safe I am in your love. In Jesus's name. Amen.

Blessings to you, my brothers and sisters in Christ.

Today's Scripture: Psalms 144:1

"Blessed be the Lord my strength, which teacheth my hands to war, and my fingers to fight."

Today's Message: When Blessing Turns into Battle

What fills your heart when a blessing turns into a battle? As we go through different seasons, we will find that some of God's gifts are followed by periods of resistance. When the struggles begin, they can sometimes target us on a deep level and hit us where we're not expecting it. But even our trials can give us hope and sharpen our awareness of His constant defense and provision. "[T]hus saith the Lord unto you, 'Be not afraid nor dismayed by reason of this great multitude; for the battle is not yours, but God's'" (2 Chronicles 20:15b).

Don't waste a minute fretting when you have a sudden deterioration of circumstances, no matter what form it takes. Bodies can be afflicted, emotions can be stirred, and minds can become confused, but God is still on the throne. All difficulties have the potential to override the joy we have found in His goodness, but we must not let them. When troubles come, we may feel as though He is no longer there, but His unceasing grace and kindness will not fail us. Though we may not always perceive it, His care for us does not cease. "It is of the Lord's mercies that we are not consumed, because His compassions fail not. They are new every morning: great is thy faithfulness" (Lamentations 3:22–23).

Conflicts reveal our vulnerabilities, but often, all that is required is for us to allow things to take their course, knowing who is fighting for us. We must focus our eyes on Jesus instead of on the conditions around us. This is the reason it was allowed to happen in the first place. He wants us to learn to look to Him and grow in faith. "[t]hough now for a season, if need be, ye are in heaviness through manifold temptations: that the trial of your faith, being much more precious than of gold that perisheth, though it be tried with fire, might be found unto praise and honor and glory at the appearing of Jesus Christ" (1 Peter 1:6b–7).

In every struggle, we must remember the blessings that preceded it but also the blessing that it is. We will sometimes be allowed to experience adverse circumstances that we may learn to lean on Him. Oftentimes, we try to fall back on our own devices when things look bleak, but seeking His way and His plan in the midst of battle is the wisest thing we can do.

After seasons of joy and sweetness, you may encounter conflict, but every battle you face will end with a time of deep relief and peace from God. *No one* is greater than the one who is in you. As we grow in understanding, we'll see that even our trials are part of His tapestry of goodness toward us. We'll come to realize that everything we are allowed to experience is for our good. We are His children, and we will find great delight in knowing deep in our hearts that we are treasured by Him. Those who belong to the Lord are in a safe haven, and our soul's rest is found only in the one who is "the same yesterday, today, and forever" (Hebrews 13:8).

Today's Prayer

Abba Father, as I come before your throne of grace, I thank you that each battle comes with greater expectation of your kindness and consolation at the end. Take this heart and seal in it the awareness of your constant goodness. Let others see that my course in this life was created by your perfect will and for my highest good. In Jesus's mighty name. Amen.

Blessings to you, my brothers and sisters in Christ.

Today's Scripture: Psalm 46:1–3

"God is our refuge and strength, a very present help in trouble. Therefore will not we fear, though the earth be removed, and though the mountains be carried into the midst of the sea; Though the waters thereof roar and be troubled, though the mountains shake with the swelling thereof."

Today's Message: Remembrance and Refuge

What is your response when the tribulations of this world find their way into your life? Our initial reaction reveals the prevailing influence on our hearts. Sometimes we try to control negative circumstances or we flee them altogether. Other times, we stand firm, resting in the remembrance of God's faithfulness and believing deeply that He will see us through. Not every test is the same, and not every response will necessarily be the same either.

His power to save has been well proven to us, and this has caused our faith to grow. But we have had wounds along the way and have developed fleshly defenses that cause us to stumble. We have seen weakness in ourselves and limited our faith in what He can do. Our heart vision is simply not wide enough to accommodate the full revelation of His power and love. Each trial we face is a gauge of our understanding, each adversity declares what we have learned, and these tests will continue to be allowed that we may learn what is in our hearts. This isn't to discourage us if we falter but to reveal *His* heart in both our victories and failures, that our vision of His love may be complete.

We can use our trials to develop a strong habit of turning to the Lord. When you are faced with unexpected difficulties, let your first action be prayer. Make a decision to practice this in every condition that presents itself. If possible, withdraw from the situation at hand and ask for the grace to know and to do what is necessary. Sometimes this simply means asking for help to center yourself on Him. Sometimes it means receiving revelation and wisdom in the moment that you may know how to navigate through a high pressure situation. Whatever is required, He is there to provide if we are willing to receive. Overcoming old behavior patterns is a process, and when we begin to taste of victory, we will be stirred to press forward and gain new ground. He is pleased when we triumph in even the slightest of battles, so be encouraged that there is no victory too small and no personal struggle too insignificant to evoke a loving response from Heaven.

Today's passage reveals a deep understanding of the extent of God's protection and provision for His people. The writer expresses what he has learned through his experiences with the Lord. He declares his confidence that no matter what happens in the natural realm, we have no reason to feel threatened: "Therefore will not we fear, though the earth be removed, and though the mountains be carried into the midst of the sea; Though the waters thereof roar and be troubled, though the mountains shake with the swelling thereof" (Psalm 46:2–3).

We live in a time when the earth strains under the weight of mounting tribulations. The sea and the waves roar, and the earth shakes in increasing waves of intensity. A call from Heaven sounds forth to the people of Earth. It is a call to seek refuge and strength, not in man, nor in the institutions of man but in God. "Give us help from trouble: for vain is the help of man. Through God we shall do valiantly: for He it is that shall tread down our enemies" (Psalm 60:11–12). The Father waits with open arms and abundant provision, ready to save and deliver all who call upon His name in truth.

Today's Prayer

Father, I thank you that you are my very present help in every trouble and that you know what I have need of before I think to ask. I pray for the grace to see this in every challenge I face. Help me to grow in faith as you reveal how great your power and love for me are. In the mighty name of Jesus. Amen.

Blessings to you, my brothers and sisters in Christ.

Today's Scripture: Philippians 2:5–9

"Let this mind be in you, which was also in Christ Jesus: Who, being in the form of God, thought it not robbery to be equal with God: But made Himself of no reputation, and took upon Him the form of a servant, and was made in the likeness of men. And being found in fashion as a man, He humbled Himself, and became obedient unto death, even the death of the cross. Wherefore God also hath highly exalted Him, and given Him a name which is above every name."

Today's Message: Broken Vessels Lead to Glory

What does it mean to be broken before the Lord? Sometimes our Father chooses to do a work in us that bypasses our lifestyles, our status, and our plans. It is a deep work of refinement and cleansing, and the more we understand it, the closer we will come to the heart of the Saviour. This is because *He* was once broken. "The cup of blessing which we bless, is it not the communion of the blood of Christ? The bread which we break, is it not the communion of the Body of Christ?" (1 Corinthians 10:16).

Our search to learn His ways will always lead us back to the cross of Calvary. We must see His cross and ours from His perspective, because the fruit of them both is eternal and beyond anything we could imagine. "Now unto Him that is able to do exceeding abundantly above all that we ask or think, according to the power that worketh in us, unto Him be glory in the Church by Christ Jesus throughout all ages, world without end. Amen" (Ephesians 3:20–21).

In order for us to move forward into all that God has for us, we must recognize that we have built-in limitations to our growth and relationship with Him. That's why it is necessary that this work be accomplished within us. Each of us has certain breaking points that will cause us to seek Him for refuge and restoration, and this is what will lead the broken to glory. Once He has touched and dismantled those hindrances in our souls that we hold so dear, we will discover new dimensions of His love, we will uncover new depths in His plans, and we will experience true wholeness and joy. "And that He might make known the riches of His glory on the vessels of mercy, which He had afore prepared unto glory" (Romans 9:23).

Are we willing to hear God's voice, to let go of whatever is necessary, and to surrender to His process? Are we willing to avoid using up precious time and energy trying to resist this vital work? "For whosoever will save his life shall lose it: but whosoever will lose his life for my sake, the same shall save it" (Luke 9:24). Possessions, power, and money do not shield us, for His power to orchestrate events is beyond our ability to think or plan for. He is searching for a servant who is willing to become *nothing* that they may gain *everything*.

Oftentimes, the world looks at the downtrodden and sees them as insignificant or useless, but God is on the throne, and He alone decides what is valuable. Only He can take what has been broken and flow through it in His mighty power. "Therefore I take pleasure in infirmities, in reproaches, in necessities, in persecutions, in distresses for Christ's sake: for when I am weak, then am I strong" (2 Corinthians 12:10).

When we see the end result and discover that it could only be arrived at through perfect wisdom and careful tenderness, we will desire nothing less than to give everything back to Him for His glory!

Today's Prayer

Abba Father, I choose to unveil everything in my heart before you. I thank you for taking what is broken and using it to complete me. Lord, you are my Saviour, and you will save me from everything that holds me back from you. Thank you for the price you paid on the cross to make me free in every way. In Jesus's name. Amen.

Blessings to you, my brothers and sisters in Christ.

Today's Scripture: Philippians 2:8–11

"And being found in fashion as a man, He humbled Himself, and became obedient unto death, even the death of the cross. Wherefore God also hath highly exalted Him, and given Him a name which is above every name: That at the name of Jesus every knee should bow, of things in Heaven, and things in Earth, and things under the earth; And that every tongue should confess that Jesus Christ is Lord, to the glory of God the Father."

Today's Message: The Power of Humility

Have you ever meditated on the truth that the greatest of all victories was won through an act of divine submission? To the world, the preaching of the cross is foolishness. But to those who have received the atonement, the cross demonstrates its mighty power in very personal and tangible ways. Love and meekness always triumph over hatred and aggression. Surrender to the God of love always brings victory over the enemy. "Be not overcome of evil, but overcome evil with good" (Romans 12:21). Humility gives place to the empowerment of the Spirit that we may deny the demands of self and walk in obedience to the one who gave everything to save us.

The world exalts natural displays of power like physical strength, riches, or material possessions, but all success in these areas is temporary and ultimately empty. The highest authority in the spirit realm is found in Christ. Everything we are and all that we accomplish is by His grace, which means it is unearned. He willingly equips us with everything we need to overcome because of His love for us and His love for those who will benefit from our victory. "Now thanks be unto God, which always causeth us to triumph in Christ, and maketh manifest the savor of His knowledge by us in every place" (2 Corinthians 2:14).

Growth in humility requires a consistent choosing to focus on the Lord, to see His greatness as we commune with Him, and to walk in truth. It also requires a dismantling of those areas of fleshly strength that are a hindrance to us. We must be patient both with the process and with ourselves as this work is accomplished within us. "But let patience have her perfect work, that ye may be perfect and entire, wanting nothing" (James 1:4).

It is great victory to gain the assurance that no matter what's happening or how much we're struggling, He is in control and working it all together for our good. It's important that we develop attitudes and mindsets that leave our hearts open to the Lord. As we cultivate purity of intent, increase in our willingness to serve, and choose to be content in all things, we will find it much easier to yield to the inner work of the Spirit. These practices and perspectives will settle us within and prevent us from pushing ahead or using manipulation to advance ourselves. They will help us to trust and unify with Him as we are brought to a higher place. "Trust in the Lord with all thine heart; and lean not unto thine own understanding. In all thy ways acknowledge Him, and He shall direct thy paths" (Proverbs 3:5,6).

Many today seek power, but God honors the meek. Many admire the strong and proud, but God chooses the weak and desperate. Many are impressed by fame and high status, but God favors the broken. "The sacrifices of God are a broken spirit: a broken and a contrite heart, O God, thou wilt not despise" (Psalm 51:17). The world worships the material and the external, but God is looking for the faithful and the humble. Consider the ways you have been blessed throughout your life and list those blessings when you're alone with Him. To truly own the fact that *all* is a work of grace is to humble yourself. Spend time today thanking Him for His goodness, rejoice that everything you have is a gift, and you will be empowered to overcome. "Humble yourselves in the sight of the Lord, and He shall lift you up" (James 4:10).

Today's Prayer

Heavenly Father, I come before you and I stand in awe of you. You have given me every reason to believe that your ways are perfect. Thank you for the abundance of grace and blessing that you have poured out upon me and for the heart of humility you are working within me. In Jesus's name. Amen.

Blessings to you, my brothers and sisters in Christ.

Today's Scripture: 2 Chronicles 20:17

"Ye shall not need to fight in this battle. Set yourselves, stand ye still, and see the salvation of the Lord with you O Judah and Jerusalem. Fear not, nor be dismayed. Tomorrow go out against them, for the Lord will be with you."

Today's Message: Victory Through Faith and Humility

Did you know that part of fighting the good fight is allowing yourself to be vulnerable so the Lord can show Himself strong? We have all been through trials that felt like they were more than we could bear, but each time of testing we enter into presents an opportunity for great victory and consolation. All that is needed is a truth-based perspective and a vertical focus.

If we are seeking a deeper and more meaningful walk with the Lord, we must recognize that the difficult periods are as necessary as the mountaintop experiences. It is our struggles that lead us to be humble and receptive to what He is saying and revealing about Himself. "That the trial of your faith, being much more precious than of gold that perisheth, though it be tried with fire, might be found unto praise and honour and glory at the appearing of Jesus Christ" (1 Peter 1:7).

As we grow, our perspective about what is important changes, and we begin to see that there's much more to the plan of God than we were aware of. He wants us to know Him in adversity and to be close to Him in the midst of battle. Knowing the peace and unconditional love of God is the greatest blessing our hearts can receive, but connecting with Him in the midst of our struggles is what causes our roots to grow deep. It's hard to grasp at first that His desire is to relate to us during times that bring negative feelings to the surface.

But when we experience His grace and mighty hand, we will hardly be able to contain our thankfulness. We will gain deep and freeing revelations as He walks through the fire with us. We will learn that every step of our journey has been saturated with His knowing provision and protection and that He does indeed walk with us and go before us.

Make Him your top priority before you start each day, set your affection on the things of Heaven, and you will discover His unwavering attention to your needs. "If ye then be risen with Christ, seek those things which are above, where Christ sitteth on the right hand of God. Set your affection on things above, not on things on the earth" (Colossians 3:1–2).

The more we focus on the Lord, the more He will be revealed to us and become our first love. Some are still searching for His path, not realizing that He greatly desires to help them find it. Some have wandered and have needed help to find their way again. None of us are strong enough to do it on our own. When we gain the revelation that it is the Father's good pleasure to give us the Kingdom, a deep rest will settle in our hearts. Humility is the simple recognition that He is our only source and that we cannot fight the battles before us without Him. Faith is the choice to shift from a focus that is earthbound to one that sees Him as He is and to let all actions flow from that vantage point. This day, choose to seek and to find victory by looking to Him alone.

Today's Prayer

Abba Father, thank you for your word of wisdom that lifts my spirit when there is no one I can turn to. Each battle and challenge that I face makes me love you more, because I know that a fresh glimpse of your glory awaits me as you bring me through to the other side. In Jesus's name. Amen.

Blessings to you, my brothers and sisters in Christ.

Today's Scripture: Ezekiel 43:2

"And, behold, the glory of the God of Israel came from the way of the east: and His voice was like a noise of many waters: and the earth shined with His glory."

Today's Message: The Union of Many Waters

Have you ever considered the multifaceted wonder of the voice of God? The closer we get to Him, the more we will discover that there is great diversity in the way He communicates with us. Sometimes He whispers gently to our hearts. Sometimes He speaks through man, for He became flesh and dwelt among us and ministers yet through His people. Whenever He speaks, He has a purpose to accomplish. The same is true of *how* He speaks. His words and the ways they are expressed are as manifold as the ears and hearts that would hear them. His fellowship with His children is specifically tailored to each heart that each would be ministered to with perfect clarity and absolute, intimate understanding.

"And I heard as it were the voice of a great multitude, and as the voice of many waters, and as the voice of mighty thunderings, saying, 'Alleluia: for the Lord God omnipotent reigneth. Let us be glad and rejoice, and give honour to Him: for the marriage of the Lamb is come, and His wife hath made herself ready'" (Revelation 19:6,7). This flood of voices from before the throne is embraced by waves of intimacy pouring over His people. This exchange will echo through the ages as our Father reveals wonders beyond wonders greater than our natural minds can conceive. No matter the degree of His love we have experienced in this life, none can fathom the extent to which He has gone to prepare a place for those who love Him. When we exhale our last breath in this world and inhale our first beyond the veil, all that is lower, all that is pain, all that has burdened us in this life will be washed away forever. It will be utterly forgotten before the flood of revelatory grace cascading over our hearts from the throne of God. "That in the ages to come He might shew the exceeding riches of His grace in His kindness toward us through Christ Jesus" (Ephesians 2:7).

The Lord does not speak in words alone. When we perceive that our circumstances have been arranged to bring about protection and provision, we have heard His voice. When someone is brought to us to offer encouragement and support in the midst of our struggles, we have heard His voice. When we notice that events have been orchestrated to lift our countenance and cause us to rise above discouragement and despair, we have heard His voice. These are the kisses of Heaven brought to us when they are needed most. These are the words of our Father who delights to speak to His children and rejoices when we understand His speech.

This day, as you go about your earthly routines, ask Him to open your ears. He is always speaking. He is always wooing you with total awareness of your every need. Allow yourself to walk with an open hand. Release every thought of what you *think* you need and trust in His heart and wisdom. He will not fail you. He will not fail to finish His work in the small, valuable portion of His Body that you are. You will stand on that day having heard the voice of many waters and will rejoice in all that is to come. "Now unto Him that is able to do exceeding abundantly above all that we ask or think, according to the power that worketh in us, unto Him be glory in the Church by Christ Jesus throughout all ages, world without end. Amen" (Ephesians 3:20–21).

Today's Prayer

Father, I thank you that you know me. I thank you that as I stand among the multitudes, you direct your word to me with full understanding of all that I am and all that I need. Lead me down the path to perfect union with you that I may join my voice to the great host before your throne. In Jesus's name. Amen.

Blessings to you, my brothers and sisters in Christ.

Today's Scripture: Zephaniah 3:17

"The Lord thy God in the midst of thee is mighty; He will save, He will rejoice over thee with joy; He will rest in His love, He will joy over thee with singing."

Today's Message: The Throne of Joy

Do you ever wonder where your path will lead when you step from this life into the next? We tend to think of Earth as a journey and Heaven as a destination, but when we stand before the Lord on that day, we will find that our journey has just begun. We will experience a new beginning and yet a continuation of every good thing He has done in us. All Kingdom purposes that have flowed through us will be extended in a purer way and on a higher plane. As we walk out His will in this world, we are being prepared for much more than we can understand. The vision that will unfold before us as we finish our course has been hidden from eternity in the heart of the Father, predestined and established before His throne of joy.

"Lord, thou wilt ordain peace for us, for thou also hast wrought all our works in us" (Isaiah 26:12). The moment the name of Jesus first passed through our lips by the Spirit, His work began, teaching and shaping, restoring and renewing, correcting and redirecting. The children He has brought forth by His grace are not afterthoughts or projects patiently upheld until we reach Heaven but expressions of the joy of His heart. He works within us, gladly shaping us into who we already are in spirit and who we will be forever. The eternal purposes of God come from a place of foresight so vast that if we gained but a taste of their depth, the appeal of this present realm would seem as bondage to us. Hand in hand, we are led forward with nothing expected but a willingness to discover and to take the next step.

"Many, O Lord my God, are thy wonderful works which thou hast done, and thy thoughts which are to us-ward: they cannot be reckoned up in order unto thee: if I would declare and speak of them, they are more than can be numbered" (Psalm 40:5). Do you know what it means to be His? Even the most spiritually mature among us have had but a taste of this. We leave nothing behind in this world but that which is contrary to us. We bring nothing with us as we part the veil but that which He has done in and through us. All is grace. All is a gift. Not grudgingly or reluctantly does He bestow the Kingdom upon His people. Joy is the rule of His house. Ours is the glad reception of everything He delights to give.

Even as the modes and mindsets of our former poverty cling to us, we are given foretastes of our hope. We are allowed glimpses into who He is, who we are, and where we are going. The greater revelation of our eternal state is not withheld from us because of His unwillingness to make it known. It is withheld because we can only know resurrection life to the degree that we have already died. This too is His work. You haven't suffered in His will because He is displeased with you. You have suffered in His will because of His zeal to accomplish your expected end and His resolve to remove everything that would hinder it. "For I reckon that the sufferings of this present time are not worthy to be compared with the glory which shall be revealed in us" (Romans 8:18).

When all that can be done in you has been done, you will pass into your inheritance and worship the Lord in your completeness. This is certain for each of His children. The light of His love for you cannot be dimmed by anything in this realm, including you. Allow this truth to make its way into your soul until your countenance is lifted to behold Him, for God is love.

Today's Prayer

Father, I have but one request, that I may see you as you are. The revelation of your joy-filled heart toward me provides all the strength needed to walk into the fullness of who I am in your Kingdom. May you reveal it to me today that I may carry it through this life and into your presence forever. In Jesus's name. Amen.

ABOUT THE AUTHORS

Michael and Julie Battaglini currently live in Rochester, Minnesota, with their dog, Mordechai. They were married in 2014, and the Father has mingled their unique combination of gifts and callings to produce a deep and rich ministry of His Spirit through them. They are involved in a home-church fellowship and have a passion to see the Kingdom of God flourish in the hearts and lives of those around them.

Each day, Julie ministers to and prays for the sick and hurting. The Lord uses her to bring healing and refreshing to those He brings across her path, some of whom have come seeking medical care in Rochester as their last hope. She receives numerous testimonies from people who tell her of the spiritual, physical, and emotional healing they have received from Him during their time in Rochester. It was in this context that the two of them were led to write letters of encouragement and exhortation to those she had prayed for and to hand them out wherever the Spirit directed them.

Michael and Julie's ministry of the written word has become a demonstration of the simplicity that God so often chooses to work through. He has continued to expand the depth and power of His anointing through them as they simply make themselves available to extend the reach of His love and kindness to His children. It has been their strong desire to model this informal approach to imparting the life and power of the Spirit that others may know that they too can discover their place in God's Kingdom.

CPSIA information can be obtained
at www.ICGtesting.com
Printed in the USA
LVHW011729141220
674147LV00004B/983